Triumphs Of Good Over Evil

By
Talissa Bee

Copyright © 2018 Talissa Bee

All rights reserved. No part of this publication may be used or reproduced in any manner whatsoever without written permission except in the case of brief quotations embodied in critical articles and reviews.

PUBLISHER'S NOTE

The individual experiences recounted in this book are true. However, in some instances, names and other descriptive details have been altered to protect the identities of the people involved.

Cover Photo by Joshua Earle

First paperback edition, 2018

Table of Contents

Introduction 1
CHAPTER ONE 8
Positive actions win enemies 8

   First minute: Friend or enemy 14
   Life is about choices 17
   It takes two to tango 20
   Anger: A battle you can win 26
   Here today, gone tomorrow 36
   First serve then deserve 42

CHAPTER TWO 47
Positive actions create charisma 47

   Only once in a lifetime 52
   Charisma starts with your mind 55
   Why smile? Why be grateful? 62
   The house of a thousand mirrors 68
   A ton of benefits of being a helper 73
   The Starting point of falling in love 76

CHAPTER THREE 78
Positive actions develop relationships 78

   The power of words 84
   It is a matter of patience 90
   A miracle of the lip balm pot 96
   A dirty laundry 100
   Half a watermelon 102
   Think the other way round 107
   Do not measure others with your ruler 111
   Release your expectations 116

CHAPTER FOUR 120
Positive actions lead to success. 120

   The tale of a lucky man...122
   A fish that can be eaten throughout the year 127
   Sincerity is the best source of trust 129
   The sheer passion and dedication can make you shine..............135
   Emotional engagement is worth the investment 141
   Goodwill brings good future..145

Epilogue 149
About the Author..157

Introduction

It happened when I was studying in grade 11. Once I heard the news of my grandfather's death, instead of crying or being in shock, I felt *nothing.*

Some people said that it is not weird since the strength of a grief response is directly related to the bond with the deceased and it may be true. Normally, kids are very fond of their grandparents because they shower a lot of love for them. But my grandparents were sort of different.

My parents and I occasionally visited them, especially on some weekends, holidays and family events. Unfortunately, it was unable to build a good relationship between my grandparents and me. An invisible wall that they chose never to breach discouraged me to approach them. We had never played together and seldom talked to each other. I never had an opportunity to get close to them.

However, when my last year of elementary school was about to begin, I got a bad news. My parents abruptly decided to move from a small city flat to a suburban house and they had no other option but to send me to live with my grandparents until I finished elementary school. They explained to me that it was hard to find a new school for me in a short time, and travel between home and my school could be really inconvenient and costly. But it would take only ten minutes with a few pennies to go to my school if I stayed at my grandparents' house. My mom said that I would have to be patient for only one year and then we could live all together again.

I could say that 'only one year' was a joyless time for me. It got awkward staying in the same house as my grandparents. With all of unfamiliar circumstances and uncomfortable sleeping situations, it could be daunting. However, I tried to adjust myself as best as a twelve-year-old girl could.

My grandmother was a little chubby, rarely smiled, and preferred to spend time inside home all day. Whereas, my grandfather was a man without an ounce of excess fat, still lean and fit in his sixtieth year. He usually went to a small coffee shop nearby since early morning, before everybody in the house could even get out of bed.

This coffee shop was on my way to school as well and sometimes I could spot him sitting at one table with a cup of coffee in front of him. His head lowered as he was reading a newspaper. Most of customers were at around the same age as my grandfather, so this could be the possible reason why going to this coffee shop became his regular routine. It was the place where he could have a drink, meet friends, and relax. And that's all I had learned about my grandparents when I lived there.

Later, my grandfather was being admitted to hospital with symptoms of lung cancer due to smoking for over 30 years. Each time my family went to visit him, I would find him lying in bed like droopy or wilted vegetables. He was able to neither move nor talk and on oxygen all the time. He had lost around 20 pounds in weight. I couldn't recall if he had a surgery or not, but he left us after two years of suffering with it.

My grandfather died when I was sixteen. It was the first death I faced. Yet, I did not feel much about his death - or so I thought. I did, actually. My eyes shed no tears not even one drop at his funeral, though. Grief takes time to hit a person's psyche and really takes a toll. I just lost the sense of it and it affected my mind in the way I'd never expected.

The next day after my family was notified of my grandfather's death, we used our pickup truck to go to hospital to bid him last goodbye. Since there was no enough room for a rear-facing seat to sit down, my older brother and I had to ride in the back of the vehicle. And it was no fun for me because the roadway was really bad at that time. There were many obstacles such as potholes or debris which caused bumps. Dust and the hot weather made matters worse.

I could do nothing except let my eyes wander down the street. Then, out of the blue, I started to feel hatred in my heart for everything and kept thinking about how fake and shallow the world was. My head was full of negative thoughts like a pile of sludge. Normally, I had been timid and modest - so how was it that I could become such aggressive and hateful for no reason?

Soon after, my rage jumped out to the surface. I began giving a dirty look at the car coming after ours. I stared right through its windshield but the sunlight didn't allow me to see the passengers. I didn't even know what gender and how old the driver was. But that couldn't stop me.

Deep down inside, I knew what I was doing was wrong, but I was unable to control myself. A cold glare and sneer continued to form on my face as if whoever in that car were the ones who sparked a flame within me and it was their faults.

It did not take a long time for them to notice a bad expression on my face and it would have pissed them off because that car began to move in the threatening way. The driver did not maintain a safe distance behind our car anymore. He or she was chasing after us and we were likely to get hit many times.

At one point, they approached our car and stopped at the hint of danger. However, I was too nasty to lose my dignity (a stupid one, of course). I refused to quit giving them a glare even though my body was getting tensed with panic and fear.

Suddenly, I became aware of the rest of my family - my dad, my mom, and my brother - no one deserved to be in a danger which was obviously triggered by my unreasonable behaviors.

With that thought, I gave in and averted my face away. I had to wait for almost ten minutes before people in that car started to calm down. Finally, they accelerated their car, overtook our vehicle, and then disappeared from my sight. I was so ashamed and guilty I could not look directly at that car when it passed by.

Instead of grief and sadness, I had experienced an amount of upsetting emotions regarding my grandfather's death and those people in that car were only victims of my anger. In other words, I just abused strangers. Although I was a teenager at that time - a period that can be best described as an emotional roller coaster and hormonal changes, it was not a reason to dump my anger on someone else. Certainly, no one likes to be mad at, especially without knowing why.

It is said that, *"How you treat others is how you invite them to treat you."* The first time I heard this quote I understood its meaning right away as it reminded me of this incident which happened nearly 20 years ago but it is difficult for me to forget. In fact, it seems to get stuck in my memory and turns out to be one of my valuable life lessons.

I have learned that if you give someone a smile, you will surely receive one in return. If you talk to other people with politeness and respect, they shall treat you in the same way.

On the contrary, if you sound aggressive or direct, they are going to offend you and it probably causes a problem in the discussion. To be successful, we all need help and everyone has something to offer. You will be surprised at how many people will be willing to support and follow you if you treat them nicely, regardless of what you have achieved or where you are in your life.

CHAPTER ONE
Positive actions win enemies

Aristotle, the legendary Greek philosopher, once said "Man is by nature a social animal." Since the early days humans stay in groups. We grow up, develop, and learn about the world around us through the filter of other people. We have created community, religion, state on the same basis that we find it secure to be in group.

The recent appearance of various social networking tools and their adoption at a virtually explosive rate nicely illustrate the strong and fundamental human desire for social belonging and interpersonal exchange.

Obviously, we relate to other people one way or another and we cannot deny the fact that there are good and bad people everywhere on the planet.

In terms of difficult people, they can be around you - in a train, on a street, in a public park, at an office, or even next door. If you are unable to free yourself from anger and disgust when you think about someone else's wrongdoing, this world is no different from a prison for you.

A following story is what really happened to John.

John is an antique shop owner. One day he went to open his shop as usual and found that a new owner who has recently taken over a coffeehouse next to his shop setup a big vertical banner display to show images of beverage menu and prices. It would be fine if this banner did not take up some spaces of John's storefront.

According to the above situation, pick the response that sounds closest to how you would likely react if you were John.

A. ...walk over to the coffeehouse and tell the owner, perhaps loudly, that you want him to remove the banner right away

B. ...create your own banner and place it up against the

coffeehouse's banner in an attempt to claim the spot that should be yours

C. ...neither say nor do anything to reproach the coffeehouse owner, but keep complaining about it incessantly to anyone who will listen

Psychologists will categorize our range of reactions including emotions by several theories, but an important part of different reactions are individual's personality types.

Those who answer A. are sort of bold and more likely to lose their temper easily. If the answer is B., they are the type of person who tends to be harsh, confrontational and not going to allow others to easily take advantage of them. And if they are passive and lack of self-confidence, they would choose C. That is a reason why people react in the different ways to the same situation.

In our life, we inevitably run into some annoying, frustrating, or aggressive people who test our patience to the max. And as a human, we have a tendency to react to them with anger. We may try to insult them, humiliate them, or hurt their feelings in return.

In this case, however, it frequently makes things worse. You will never produce good results when you express anger by yelling, hitting, or breaking things.

Believe it or not, you can make bad situations better without getting even with difficult people or punishing them. And John is one such example.

Although John was really upset with the inconsiderate behavior of the new owner of coffeehouse, he tried to calm down and continue to do his own work. Next day, the banner was still in the exact same position but John was quite busy with some errands to run, so he had no time to give it much attention. He asked his employee to take care of the shop during his absence.

After few hours, John got his errands finished and ready to go back to the shop. Then he noticed the rows of booths selling a variety of fresh fruits and vegetables of every color which stirred up his eager to taste. He stopped to make a purchase and then a strange idea suddenly entered his head. It told him to buy some fruits for the coffeehouse owner.

'That's crazy.' he said to himself.

There was a moment's hesitation before John decided to listen to it at last.

When John offered fruits to the coffeehouse owner who was a man with mustache and glasses, John could clearly see an awkward expression on his face. The man refused to take them but John insisted that it was his pleasure and since they had opened their shops next to each other, they were like neighbors. They could share things, keep an eye on each other's properties, and provide assistance when necessary.

After hearing John's reasons, the coffeehouse owner, whose name was later revealed as Ricky, finally accepted the gift and started to talk to John with more ease. The conversation proceeded to flow naturally and made them know that they had a lot in common. Actually, they felt as if they were talking to an old friend.

Next day, John came to open his shop as usual and, to his surprise, the banner had disappeared. He looked around but was not able to find it - which should satisfy him because his storefront was no longer obstructed by it.

It turned out that John wondered what happened and went to the coffeehouse to inform Ricky that his banner was gone. However, Ricky said, with a slight bit of guilt on his face, that he was afraid that the banner was blocking pedestrians' visibility of John's products so he moved it to a new designated position in his own shop already.

John had really expected nothing when he gave fruits to Ricky. He also made no mention of the banner at all in their first conversation. Ricky had stopped stealing the space of John's storefront, though.

People typically do not want to be friends with those who hope them to change but their behaviors are likely to change, particularly into more positive ones, when a friendship relationship grows among themselves, or when one considers another individual as "friend".

First minute: Friend or enemy

Friendship is one of the most important aspects of human's life. So important, in fact, that it has been proven that social relationships can influence chemicals in our brains.

I guess you might have similar experiences that you just feel happy and warm when your friend texts you, gives you a phone call or surprises you by showing up at your front door to see how you are doing or to get together and have fun.

And it can feel like the end of the world when you get in a fight with your friends or lose them. Having the support of friends and family can counteract feelings of loneliness, inadequacy, and other states associated with depression.

In addition, being social can extend life expectancy, whereas lonely people are more likely to die early and have higher chances of heart disease or stroke as a recent study by the University of York has found.

Making someone your friends really takes effort and for some people it will take a while before they can consider you their friend. But it is very surprising how easy it is to make someone your enemy.

Sometimes people simply decide to turn another into an enemy out of fear, disagreement, or just an unreasonable and envious hatred. Throughout your life, you will be always finding people who are happy to hang out with you and the ones who offend you for no reason.

Nevertheless, some people seem to attract more friends than foes and it is all because of the way they think, speak, and act. They give out positive vibes of openness and consideration. They have no problem compromising, forgiving, and helping others when being asked. Generally, they are viewed as a reliable and kind person, which open the door to friendship.

In the meantime, there are a significant number of people who just do not know how to build good relationships with others. They have never stopped to think how their actions, words, and decisions may affect other people's feelings.

These people seem insensitive, self-centered, and inflexible. They have even lost enough to be not aware that they are annoying others. On the other hand, they start whining immediately when they are treated badly and believe that they are a victim of social bullying without looking back at themselves.

There are several tips and techniques out there to make friends and win over your enemies. But if you examine them in detail, you will realize that they are based on just single common concept - *doing good deeds for the benefit of others*. The finding that positive behavior begets positive behavior and negative behavior begets negative behavior is not exactly new.

Good acts - acts of kindness, generosity and cooperation - can spread just as easily as bad. Start with your own self, adjust your attitudes, connect to your personal goodwill, and then make it hard for people to disrespect you or hate you. This is how you can bring untold amounts of happiness, friendship, and positive changes - not only to yourself but also to everyone else around you.

Life is about choices

The first step to turn enemies into friends is to understand that life is just a series of decisions we make and there are many situations where you have to face two or more choices.

You are perhaps unable to control the world or what happens to you, but you can certainly control how you choose to react to it, which will shape your future and in some way change your life forever.

Every decision and every choice, from what you eat, to where you work and live, and especially the people you spend your time with, in fact, everything in your life, business and personal, exists because you first made a choice about it. We do not suddenly become fat, sick, or short of money but they are the result of tiny choices we have made along the way.

Of course there are different types of choices; some are easy to make, while others are more difficult. The best way to make the right choice, especially when it affects a major aspect of your life, is to give yourself some time to weigh carefully each option, ask what works for you, what gives you the desired results, and then choose accordingly.

In the meantime, you are likely to make a bad decision when you feel rushed, overwhelmed, angry, or tired, which frequently not only leads to unsatisfactory outcomes but also makes you regret later.

You tend to handle the situation at hand more poorly when your negative emotions have been triggered and there are a large number of examples out there showing what trouble people may bring upon themselves when they have chosen choices influenced by anger or depression.

With the rapid development of science and technology nowadays, everything spreads quickly across the globe and bad acts of individuals -- acts of rudeness, violence and aggression -- are no exception. They can destroy a first impression, reduce credibility, diminish reputations, and create an increase in expenditures. Overall, they have a hugely damaged impact of their personal and professional life as a result of making impulsive decisions.

No matter what happens, do not make decisions when you are in an emotional state. It can help if you step back, take a deep breath and wait a few hours or days to let your intense emotions cool down before confronting a situation or a person that makes you unhappy.

Certainly, life sometimes can be tough but the power to control your destiny is in your own hands through your choices - like William Ernest Henley's closing words from his famous poem 'Invictus' that "*I am the master of my fate, I am the captain of my soul.*"

If you choose to not take a responsibility, you simply give away all the power you have and your life is about be blown like a leaf in the wind. You are the only person who can determine your future and therefore choose wisely.

It takes two to tango.

Two cats are walking down a path on opposite sides; one is white, the other is yellow. When they come closer, the yellow cat starts to hiss while his ears are flattening, back is arching and tail is fluffing out in a poufy plume, as if he is ready to attack the white cat if necessary.

The white cat pauses moving but show no fear or anxiety. They keep watching on each other for a moment before the yellow cat backs off and slowly walks away.

In many cases, when there is a confrontation between cats and one of them runs away, it appears that he will be chased after and the catfight is almost inevitable. On the other hand, if that cat chooses to remain calm, the other will be afraid of getting closer and picking a fight.

It is clear that there is no cause without an effect on this earth. Every action you take and every decision you make have consequences and will produce specific results in your life.

Someone perhaps cuts you off in a traffic jam or steals your parking space, and you feel angry. However, an argument will never start if you choose to let it go.

Conflicts always require two people and reactions between each other. No one can pick a fight with you if you do not participate as Sir Isaac Newton's third Law of Motion states that "For every action, there is an equal and opposite reaction."

For example, you are married but there is this man or woman who is trying to approach you personally and flirt with you. If you feel proud of yourself and enjoy the excitement, chances are you end up cheating on your wife or husband and, believe me, there is nothing hidden that will not be at some pointed revealed.

On the other hand, you will never get into trouble or regret later if you keep your distance from the seducer and run away from the circumstances that will ignite your inappropriate desires. While this is an extreme example, it serves to illustrate the point very well that '*it takes two to tango.*'

The same goes for smoking. A cigarette cannot increase your risk of getting a lung disease if you just hold it in your hand or put it between your teeth. You give it a permission to harm your health only when you light it up and inhale the smoke.

As this world is getting filled with temptations, you will encounter many distractions, trials, and tribulations to ruin the pride of your life. The trick is to work your way through deceptions, always follow your vision, and say 'No' instantly and emphatically. It is all about self-control.

You cannot control the things that happen to you much of the time, and you certainly cannot control how other people act. The only thing you can control is your response and this response matters. You can respond to the same event with anxiety or anger, or you respond with calmness and intelligent manner.

In our daily life, there is a good chance that we will experience rudeness, insults, and negative behaviors all the time. A group of people or even a stranger could have spoken harsh words that hurt us so much it tears us down emotionally and mentality. They cut through us like a knife and left a wound in our heart.

The strange but true fact is that we tend to stab ourselves with this knife over and over again even though those toxic people have long gone or even have forgotten what they have said or done to us. We inflict pain upon ourselves by repeatedly thinking, complaining, and whining about their mean words and actions, hoping that they will treat us more nicely or say that they are sorry.

However, in many cases, it is hopeless. Yet, we found ourselves crying at unexpected times while wondering what is wrong with them, why they have been so cruel, and so forth. The typical end result of doing so is a feeling of weakness to effectively deal with the situation.

Certainly, you get upset when someone yells at you or makes fun of you because you are not robot-like beings who can immediately press a button to shrug off other people's insults and accusations. You have feelings and every right to feel.

However, it is a destructive feeling if you let them hurt you. You may lose a few nights of sleep, have dark circles under your eyes, and have an eating problem. You fail to see that the pain you feel right then has nothing to do with them anymore.

If you try to seek someone or something to take a responsibility of how bad you feel, you will be never able to free your pain. You are just fanning the fire instead of putting it out. Nobody can rob you of happiness or force you to be in pain if you do not accept it by yourself.

It is you who open the door to allow them to come in and hit you. You are the one in charge of your emotions. So whatever the situation, you have the power to alter the dynamics.

It definitely requires time and practice to develop a barrier between the onrush of primal feelings and the rationality to recognize that you have a choice to feel and react the other way.

But, like every other skills, once you start practicing, you will be getting better at it. What to do is to be constantly aware of your thoughts, especially when they begin wandering in the past and provoking negative emotions from what other people have said or done to you so that you can control or stop them from affecting your mind.

This is one of the reasons why being mindful is a skill worth learning. It can help you to acknowledge a wild storm in your head and bring you back to the present moment. If you do not make excuses and keep your practice alive, you will be surprised how easier and more quickly you can clear your mind of negative thoughts than ever.

Anger: A battle you can win

Nowadays, everyone talks about being self-dependent, taking care of oneself, loving oneself, and so forth. Everybody is trying to be self-dependent in this race and they would do anything for their own benefit. But some of them do not realize the difference between being self-dependent and being selfish. They then become an annoying people instead of inspiring people.

No matter how hard you try to avoid unreasonable and inconsiderate people, you still find them around you, everywhere and every time. They may be your neighbor who likes to make loud noise during the middle of the night, your coworker who always hands you their work to complete or someone who parks his car in front of your house and blocks half of the entrance.

You cannot help, of course, feeling angry. You want to yell at them and even attack them in order to teach them a lesson. But it turns out that the first person who gets hurt is your own self.

When you feel overwhelmed by rage, your whole body and mind structure will be poisoned by it. Your muscles tense up, your blood pressure increases, your breath gets faster, and your sense of hearing becomes quite acute.

Research shows that people who have a shorter temper than others are likely to put their heart at great risk and suffer from skin problems such as rashes, wrinkles, acnes and dark spots. They also look way older than they actually are.

Despite several disadvantages of anger, it does not mean you are not allowed to feel angry when being taunted or goaded. Anger, like any emotion, is a part of human nature.

Long before, anger is useful for potential survival situations, as it pumps your body with adrenaline and gets you ready to run or to stand your ground. But human life is rarely threatened by such situations today and what typically makes you mad is feeling of powerless to what seems unfair.

Actually, the problem is not anger itself, but that most repulsive of human behaviors anger turns into. We have a tendency to lose our mind when we are angry and what we crave is revenge. In fact, some people believe that revenge is the only way to make them feel good again.

When someone wrongs them, they react outwardly with violent behaviors by furiously yelling, saying hurtful things, or damaging whatever within their reach. They feel satisfied in punishing or causing harm to those who have made them suffer.

However, psychologists have another idea. It is not pleasure or happiness when you can get even with those difficult people but it is a satisfaction in exposing aggressive and disruptive behaviors. It is also one of defense mechanism which does not boost your level of endorphins but stimulate the functions of amygdala in your brain instead. And the more you indulge in anger and this false satisfaction, the higher chance you have of getting a psychological problem.

Explosive anger is almost always destructive in one way or another and whatever you feel is not an excuse for behaving badly. Winning an argument can make it seem like you are smarter and stronger than the other person but a constant desire to win a fight is not healthy in the long term.

Many people have ended up ruining relationships, losing a job or even being put in jail because they did not know how to deal with their anger properly. Let me give a real life story as an example to illustrate this point.

Chris was a kind of quick-tempered university student. He had a girlfriend who was in her senior year of high school and lived a two hour drive apart. Much like a long distance relationship, they did not get to see each other as often as they would like to.

One day Chris called his girlfriend and asked where she was. She replied that she was hanging out at her friend's house. It was getting dark outside, so Chris told her to get back home for her own safety but she did not listen to him.

With worry, Chris decided to drive across town to pick her up by himself. When he almost reached the place, he called her again to let her know but she said that she had moved to another friend's house. Chris went there to find her but discovered later that she was not there either. Having no other choice, he called his girlfriend's mother and received the answer that they were having dinner together at a restaurant.

Chris got as confused as upset and felt like he was being fooled by his girlfriend. After a few hours of searching, he still did not know where exactly his girlfriend was. Finally, he parked his car in front of her house and waited until he saw her coming.

He got out of his car and started yelling at her out of frustration. He abused her with very harsh words, over and over again, without noticing her face that grew paler and paler.

He asked why she had to lie to him and why she did not say something. Suddenly, his mouth dropped when she quietly handed a beautifully-wrapped present to him.

It turned out that she wanted to be the first person to wish him a happy birthday and give him a gift. But it was him who ruin her plan and his own birthday surprise. The worse thing was, she was too angry to forgive him and then they broke up.

It may be difficult to resist an urge to explode at somebody or something when your blood is boiling, but surely beyond your ability.

When negative emotions arise and you are struggling to push through them. Pause whatever you are doing. Close your eyes, take a few deep breaths, count to ten, go for a walk or grab a cool drink. These strategies can help you shift your focus and regulate the *'temperature'* inside you.

You can then choose how to express it, or not to express it at all, in accordance with your rational assessment of what any given situations calls for.

You perhaps have heard about people who are classified as a calm person. They always stay positive and reasonable even though they are being disturbed by other people's bad behaviors. Don't they feel anything? You may wonder.

In fact, they do. Sometimes a lot. But they are conscious of how they are feeling and never let themselves get caught up in their own emotions. That is why they can lift themselves way above all negativity.

Generally, anger is not something that you can simply control or stop right away but it is something that you can acknowledge once it arises. The moment you recognize that anger swirls inside you is the moment you gain the power to alleviate it or even release it.

You will then find yourself becoming calmer and more capable of re-evaluating the situation from a reasonable, adult perspective before making any decisions. In most cases, your anger, bitterness and resentments will give place to understanding, forgiveness and peace.

While getting your mind off of what is bothering you may seem not viable, that is not truly the case. The mind is pliable and flexible; it can be trained.

Do not expect yourself to not feel angry, but expect yourself to be aware of your emotional state. If you keep trying and remaining mindful, you will get better at handling the intense heat of rage that burns within you.

No good comes out of having a fight with other people. It will only destroy you, both physically and mentally. Meanwhile, having a fight with anger causes you many benefits and leaves you feeling much better.

One day this battle will come to an end - without a winner and a loser. The certain payoff is that anger can no longer dominate your psyche or persona and you are, as a result, changing yourself from a slave to a master of your own emotions.

Here today, gone tomorrow

If you do not feel well for one week, you will find that what you actually care is your health and family, not money. If you are bedridden for a month, you will realize that money is as important as your health and family. But if you have a serious illness for a half year, you will be ready to trade whatever you own - money, property, social status, and fame - for your wellness.

Without your health, nothing else really matters. I have heard a lot of this common knowledge but I never truly understand it until I have experienced it myself.

In May 2015, I was diagnosed with Guillian Barre syndrome - a rare but serious disorder in which your body's immune system attacks your nerves. Some people developed it after getting the flu but that was not my case. It started with tingling sensations behind my ears once in a while and a slight numbness in my legs.

At first I thought it must be fatigue even though there was no obvious cause for the sensation. However, it was getting worse when time passed by. I felt like a thousand tiny needles were poking my feet endlessly and I had difficulty in walking and standing.

I could not get any sleep because of the intense pain. It was the pain that made me shake, whimper, and writhe all the night. Next morning I quickly went to see a physician and he said that maybe I had stayed in the same position for too long which caused inflammation in my muscles. I took medicine for about one week and my condition seemed to get better.

Before I felt happy about the recovery, I began having the problem of speaking. My facial muscles became a bit numb and less responsive. It concerned me but I still did not go to see the doctor until I was not able to smile, frown or wink anymore.

Finally, I was hospitalized for the first time in my life. Another physician told me that most patients with Guillian Barre syndrome lost their ability to control movement but my case was different in which a virus did not affect my whole body but just my face. Still, it caused me a lot of frustration as well as irritation when talking and chewing turned out to be a difficult thing to me.

After spending seven days in hospital, the doctor decided to send me home after there was no sign of dangerous complications from infection. However, I still needed to go back to the hospital every day to undergo an intensive course of electrical stimulation therapy for my affected facial muscles until I could fully restore facial expression and function back.

Subsequently I had lost eight pounds in one week and felt very weak. I walked at a pace that was quite different from my natural speed and although I tried to pick up the pace, my body did not allow me to. Many people were rushing past me; the way their heels hit the ground was very forceful - like I used to. Then I found myself asking why people were in such a hurry that they were willing to wreck their feet every step they took.

When we were young, we obsessed over being cool and popular because it was the way that we could feel liked or accepted. As we get older, we are busy with making money and, for many of us, what it means to be "happy" evolves into something called "wealth".

We tend to let marketing and advertising influence our purchase decisions and lifestyle choices. They affect the way we dress, the types of house we buy, the model of car we own, and much more.

Most of the time, we chase our endless desires, worry about what other people think of us, and get upset or depressed over little things that are not really important in life. We lose ourselves in this mess and live as if we are immortal.

You have probably heard one of famous quotes from Leo Tolstoy, "If we kept in mind that we will soon inevitably die, our lives would be completely different. If a person knows that he will die in a half hour, he certainly will not bother doing trivial, stupid, or, especially, bad things during this half hour."

That is the honest truth. Things, in the broadest sense, including emotions, only matter because you set value on them. You label them as major or minor depending on how you determine their values, and then get attached to them. That is a reason why some things matter so much to you and so little to others. But when you are going to draw your last breath, nothing really matters.

One thing I have witnessed during my hospitalization is that everyone can suffer from health problems no matter their race, gender, and age - from infants to the elderly. As cliché as it sounds, sickness and death are unavoidable.

Why do you have to care about work deadlines, annual bonuses, and other people's behaviors if you are going to die? Every setbacks, obstacles, failures, disagreements, and unwanted emotions will become easier to accept when you can remind yourself that "*everything is temporary.*" What you have worked for and try to hold on so hard will change, break down or turn to dust. It is just a matter of time. All kinds of everything have an expiration date.

When you think of life in terms of temporariness, you will be more likely to cherish the present moment and stop getting overly attached to a certain person, an object or even your own emotions.

Actually, attachment is the root of all painful feelings and holding a grudges from the past is a perfect waste of today's happiness. Time is irretrievable; once it is gone or wasted, you can never get it back. Life must get much happier when you learn to let go and forgive. As soon as you forgive someone, you are making a promise not to hold the unchangeable past against your present self.

Do not wait until your body is in poor condition or it is too late to realize the real value of your life. Nothing lasts forever and no one knows when death visits each of us.

However, this is not a reason you have to be hopeless and irresponsible. You need to try as hard as you can to find the things that do matter in your life. The key is to not waste your time and energy on getting stuck in your mind that just throws negative thoughts around you and bring yourself more suffering. This is your life, so you better make the best of it.

First serve then deserve

I have heard many tales from friends and family about how their neighbors could be rude, ruthless and uncaring. In fact, statistics show that many thousands of people around the world have claimed to suffer with 'noisy' or 'nasty' neighbors. It can become a nightmare if you live next door to bad pet owner, loud music fanatics or late-night partiers.

Jennifer encountered the same kind of problem too but, in her case, it was not her neighbors. She had peacefully lived in her house several years as her neighbor on one side was a single man and the house on the other side was unoccupied.

However, her simple happiness vanished after the man decided that his house needed some repairs. And it became the most miserable time of the year for Jennifer as soon as the construction began. Its presence affected her in a rich variety of ways. The noises drifting up from the site jostled her awake every morning while her place was very dusty.

What really irritated her was that construction workers were inconsiderate and thoughtless. They always threw trash out the second story window which often landed on Jennifer's yard – whether it was food waste, cigarette butts, and plastic bags with filthy rubbish. Even construction debris such as scrap wood and broken bricks could be seen all the time as well, causing not only dirt but also health hazards and injury risk.

Jennifer had tried many ways - sending a note, approaching the construction workers face to face with her complaints, and calling the police. The situation got better for a few days, then bad again as if these construction workers had trouble with short-term memory.

Nothing improved and it almost sent her over the edge until her friend came over to her house one day. Jennifer could not help but talk about her problem with him. Instead of feeling sorry for her, he suggested that she should take a kind and amiable approach or make friends with construction workers.

At first, Jennifer thought that it was a joke but soon realized that he was serious. His advice left her at a loss for words. She did not understand why she needed to be nice to people who seemed never care what they had done to her. However, she had no choice but to give it a try.

Since then Jennifer changed the way she had reached construction workers. She started to smile at them and give them food or drinks or other such gift from time to time. Certainly, she felt so awkward about doing so, meanwhile, it was obvious that construction workers doubted her intentions.

However, with some reluctance, they eventually accepted what she had offered which could be interpreted as a positive sign that the situation between them was not completely hopeless.

After a few weeks, they began to treat Jennifer in a less formal manner and no longer look uncomfortable when she was with them. It was around this time that she politely asked them if they could be careful when they were managing trash or rubbish so that it would not end up in her yard. The result was as good as expected. They were very cooperative and pleasant to help.

Dealing with the wrong kind of people is never easy because nobody likes to receive criticisms or complaints even if they are true. If your boss, co-worker, or neighbor starts causing problems, it does not mean you have to give up your job or move to another area. You just need some effective strategies and thoughtful gestures.

Giving is one of the most powerful principles which can generate feelings of gratitude in others and chances to turn enemies into friends. We can probably all agree that we always feel good when receiving a gift - whether it is just a small cup of coffee or a handmade card - because it shows that someone thinks about us and loves us enough to spend time and effort to get the present for us.

In fact, everyone wants to be liked and feel special. It is a common need of human beings. You experience the positive feelings of high self-esteem and self-importance when you believe that other people like, respect, and admire you. In the meantime, you see yourself in better light when you are making a contribution of some kind. You feel even happier when you give away without asking anything in return.

Many studies back this up, and it is one of the reasons why many people as well as billionaires like Warren Buffett and Bill Gates donate their fortunes to charity. Overall, the simple act of giving can create positive emotions among the giver and the receiver.

As you see, the method that both John and Jennifer had employed to deal with their 'possible enemies' is giving. What they gave was not only about food, but they also first offered friendship and generosity to those people. Therefore, it is not surprising that John and Jennifer received what they gave. That is the beauty of giving.

Giving does not mean just to spend money or donate an object. You can give your time to a lonely person, kind words to a lost soul, and knowledge to make someone's life better. However, it is necessary to understand that not everyone is going to give back to you what you have given, so do not attempt to make it mutual when you give something to someone.

The key is to give away without expecting anything back, and that includes emotions, hugs, payments, or public praise. You just need to let the Law of Cause and Effect work its magic. Believe it or not, whatever you send into the universe comes back. It will be definitely returned to you one way or another, whether you are asking for it or not.

CHAPTER TWO
Positive actions create charisma

You look at a map in your hand, trying to find a place in the country you have first visited. You have no idea where you are. In fact, you completely get lost. You lift your head, glance around, and then find two men sitting at a bus stop. You walk towards them who immediately notice you. One is looking at you with kind eyes and small smile while the other who has a stern expression on his face is frowning at you.

If you need to ask for directions from them, whom do you approach first? Certainly, it must be the man who looks friendly because you feel much more at ease to start a conversation with.

Most of people think that charisma is only about appearance, and that is a kind of misunderstanding about charisma. Physical attractiveness has something, but not everything, to do with charisma.

You can find many people out there who are not beautiful or handsome but extremely charming. It is a matter of personality, not so much of looks.

The first thing you notice about charismatic people is that they radiate positive energies most of the time. They are stable, reliable, cheerful, open, and honest. They make people comfortable around them and always show obvious pleasure in helping and sharing. They respect other people's opinions and never speak or act out of excessive egoism or jealousy. They also have a strong passion and believe in their abilities, their knowledge, and their worth. That is what makes them charming.

Charisma can shine through beauty and/or personality. Some people are charming because of their skills in making great conversation. They know when to speak and to listen. Some people are charming because they are sincere and always show what kind of person they really are.

Actually, the key to charisma lies beneath the way you interact with other people and kindness plays the major part of it. When you genuinely care for others, you are opening up the chance for yourself to meet respect, admiration, and even love.

Someone I knew has experienced this herself. Her name is Mali. She is an average woman who is not very interested in makeup and clothing. She was in her late twenties at that time when she decided to book a bus tour from Bangkok to upcountry. It was a one day trip which enabled her to observe, sightsee, and visit gorgeous temples. On the travel date, Mali found that all 47 seats were occupied and a lot of tourists aged 60 and older.

She was seated in the second row of the motor coach behind a couple who were about the same age as her grandparents. The wife was a small, timid woman whereas her husband seemed to be blunt and self-centered.

During a journey, the driver had run a movie via the thirteen inch TV screen which was located in the front of the bus. However, the picture and sound stopped after playing about thirty minutes, causing the old man to verbally express his frustration out loud. Although the driver informed him that there was a problem with the DVD player, the old man looked upset and kept complaining for a little while.

It was quiet on the bus as many of passengers simply chose to stare out the windows until the bus reached a destination. A handful of people had gathered in the aisle to get off. Mali stood up and followed others before noticing that the old man was stepping down the stairs after her. He seemed to have difficulty with walking, so Mali asked him to take her by the arm and assisted him to climb out of the coach.

She carefully helped him walk to a chair and placed him into a sitting position. The old man looked at her and said nothing. He did not even thank her but it was fine for Mali. She just enjoyed the rare opportunity to relax and take a stroll around the place.

Before it was time to return to Bangkok, Mali got surprised when the wife of the old man came up to her and randomly asked her about her name, age, and career. Despite being confused, Maki had no problem giving her an answer.

It was revealed later that the couple was really touched by Mali's kindness and they would like to introduce her to their son who was few years older than her and single. They hoped to see if there is long-term relationship potential.

A small action of kindness is not always so small to those in need and it really does bring gratitude out of others. In short, selflessness is one of beautiful character traits to have if you want to become charming.

The good news is that these traits are not given by birth but they can be learned and acquired through practice. The actions you take each day can become a part of your personality and improve your interactions with everyone around you. There are obvious evidences that charismatic people are some of the most successful and likable individuals out there and, of course, you can be one of them.

Only once in a lifetime

There is a Japanese proverb, *"Ichigo ichie"* which literally means "one time, one meeting". The term is originated by Sennorikyu (1522 - 1591), the great master of tea ceremony, and usually introduced in the traditional Japanese tea ceremony to remind the participants that this meeting will never happen again.

No matter how much effort they put in, they are unable to organize the meeting to be exactly the same as previous one. In other words, it cannot be repeated or replicated again.

Thus, the host must do his best to ensure that every guest receives great care and the meeting serves its purpose. The guests, for their part, shall be cautious and watchful before speaking or taking actions; meanwhile, treat each other as well as the host with respect, gentleness, and kindness.

In our lifetime, we meet many people: some we know for a lifetime, others only briefly. Every single day we walk down the street, get on a bus, or enter a supermarket, we always encounter people, even perfect strangers. There is a high possibility that we will not see them again for the rest of our life, but it does not mean that there is no chance at all.

This is why you should pay attention to your surroundings and people around you with a sense of appreciation, no matter who they are - a bellboy, a gas station attendant, a cashier, a waiter or a waitress, a housekeeper, or a security guard.

Keep in mind that everything in this world is uncertain. Individuals you have known in passing, talked or interacted with today may become a famous and rich person the next time you meet them. He or she may give you a favor when you need it most or become your biggest supporter in the future. Each encounter, therefore, is unique in its own way and to be cherished.

Today's gathering, today's coffee talk, or today's dinner date will never happen again in the same way. Although you meet this person several times, you are unable to create the same moment and feelings in him or her as previous ones.

You can start having enriched moments of your life everyday by treating everyone like it is the first and last time you meet them, valuing every such encounter you get in life, and appreciating other people for what they have done or said.

The reality is that your small nods, smiles, polite manners, compliments and magic words like "thank you" or "please" can increase other people's self-esteem and cause them to like themselves more. And the better you make them feel, the more impressions you gain from them. As a result, they will find you more attractive and enjoy your presence.

Charisma starts with your mind

"We can only give away to others what we have inside ourselves." - Dr. Wayne W. Dyer

When it comes to charisma, it is often easy to recognize but difficult to explain. Many people hold the false belief that it is something you are born with, a mysterious trait that cannot be developed or cultivated. The truth is, only by mastering a state of mind can anyone become a more charismatic person. Actually, charisma is closely related to happiness in many ways.

The charming people out there are people who usually have a higher state of happiness than others. They are also full of inner peace, a deep sense of inward acceptance, and kindness. That potent mix naturally makes people around them feel welcome, energized, and comfortable.

Whether knowingly or unknowingly, we are always searching for happiness for our whole lives. And that is the reason why we find happy and cheerful people attractive. However, we can only give what we have.

A genuine smile, a heartfelt gesture, and a warm movement can be brought about by only positive thoughts and feelings. I know this statement is repeated so often, but it is true. You will not be able to give someone money if you are broke. You cannot help and take care of others unless you can take care of yourself first. Likewise, you are unable to share happiness with others unless you are happy first.

One of my co-workers was usually lively, friendly, and talkative. A smile always appeared on her face as her sense of humor often generated a bright mood among us. But then we started to notice a change in her behaviors. She grew distant, talked less, and seemed to get angry easier and quicker than before. We were left without any clue what to do and, as a result, we avoided getting close to her as much as possible.

Several months went on this way until she stopped acting strange and turned to be the person who could easily smile and laugh with us again. Despite confusion, we were all glad and relieved that things got back to normal.

It was revealed later that she had been struggling to make her debt payments on time as her costs went up dramatically in the past months - mortgage, living expenses, and her son's tuition fees. But lately she had some breathing space and could gradually take control of her finances.

Although she had tried to keep the problem to herself along the way, pain was obvious. In fact, there are many people who tend to conceal or disguise their emotions, especially when they are hurt and distressed. But emotions and feelings - either positive or negative - are a form of energies which cannot be faked.

We are unable to *completely* hide our real feelings no matter how hard we try. They will spread out and affect people around us at some point like a thin faint line of light or smell leaking through the gap of the closed door. This is why we can tell if someone is delighted, breezy, sad, tense or upset without even asking.

Do not forget to be happy if you wish to make people want you and find you attractive. It is simple this way. However, when it comes to happiness, there are a lot of people who think that they would be happy if they only had a large sum of money, a big house, a new car, a nice job, a right partner.

The external factors -- either people or material things -- do actually have a significant effect on our level of happiness. But this happiness is not long lasting as it ends the moment you notice that the person or the thing that you let yourself be bound up entirely with begins to change.

If you need someone or something else to become happy, you will get controlled and mentally imprisoned by them. As a result, you will be never able to find real and long term happiness.

Remember that no one and nothing can be responsible for your own happiness. You need to stop looking for it outside of yourself and realize that *you* are in charge of your life and emotions. Start with being able to be happy by yourself.

From my experience, I found that meditation is the most powerful method that can help you create happiness within yourself, focus more on living in the present, and heal your negative emotions such as anxiety, worry, sadness, and so forth. Actually, it has a positive effect on both your entire physical and mental state. This fact is supported by an overwhelming amount of research.

Whenever you are wallowing in your problems or hurt feelings, just leave everything behind for a while and spend time concentrating on the depth and pace of your breath. This is called 'mindful breathing' practice.

At first, you may find it difficult to sit still and watch your breath. Certainly, it is not an easy task. It requires discipline, determination, and a lot of effort. But if you keep practicing it, you will get rewards that are worth it.

You will feel happy in the way you have never felt before and this happiness is not dependent on external sources which always leave you yearning for more. It is happiness that you can cultivate by yourself anywhere and anytime throughout your life.

At the end, you will be able to share some percent of your happiness to other people which makes them feel good in your presence. With this, you make yourself a more likable person.

Why smile? Why be grateful?

Have you given a smile to a person you are talking to today? Have you said thank-you to someone to show how grateful you are for them lately? Smile and saying thank you are both small actions but their power are tremendous.

Surprisingly, most of people do not smile or express gratitude enough when they are growing up even though these two little simple things can impact their day in the most amazing way.

Marisa is living in Thailand. She had learned driving a car and prepared for her first driver's license test. The test consists of 3 parts: the physical tests, the theory test and the practical tests accordingly.

The physical tests will check your color blindness, reaction time test for a stop light, depth perception, and peripheral vision. For the theory test, there are 50 multiple choice questions and the pass mark is 90% or 45 correct answers to pass. Marisa could achieve both the physical tests and the theory test the first time round.

After that came the last and most important test – actually driving a car. In a controlled environment, you are required to drive straight forward and reverse through a set of traffic cones, parallel park by changing gears no more than 7 times, and park not more than 25cm from a curb and within 30 feet of a stop sign.

Cameras and sensors are used to monitor and assess a person's driving ability, which means mistakes - any mistakes - are not acceptable.

Curb parking proves to be the most challenging and difficult test as many people repeatedly failed this test, including Marisa. The first time she had taken the test ended up stopping her car too far away from the stop sign and the second time turned out that she failed to get close to the curb as well as the stop sign when she parked. She already failed her road tests twice.

And then came the third time, Marisa really felt discouraged and worried. At the station, she met an official who was a woman in her forties. She asked Marisa for documents to prove her identity as a normal procedure.

After all this time, Marisa had never smiled at officials when she drove a car to the driving test stations because she was too nervous and overwhelmed.

But something in her gut told her that she should relax and pay full attention to the person in front of her, so Marisa politely greeted the official with a smile when she averted her eyes from papers in her hand and stared at Marisa's face. The woman did not smile back; in fact, she gave Marisa a bit strange look.

However, seconds later, she started to give Marisa some advice about driving near the curb to pass the test. Although Marisa already knew those tips very well, she nodded and softly said "alright" and "thank you" over and over while holding a small smile throughout the conversation.

Then the test began. Marisa tried to let her car roll as slowly as possible whereas the official was still standing at the starting line and watching her. Suddenly, to her surprise, Marisa heard her say in a loud voice, "Go straight!" when she seemed to make it right, and again "Too close!" when Marisa turned the steering wheel towards the curb too much.

It appeared that the official went out of her way to help Marisa to park along a curb successfully, which she really appreciated. She finally passed the test.

Do not get me wrong. I am not telling you that Marisa obtained her driver's license only because this official gave her the favor but it is because she had spent a lot of time practicing curb parking before taking the test as well. After all, this true story shows that a smile and expressions of gratitude have special powers.

As Dale Carnegie said, "The expression one wears on one's face is far more important than the clothes one wears on one's back." A smile is extremely important when it comes to first impressions; meanwhile, it requires a minimum of thought and effort.

Smiling when you first meet someone will indicate to the other person that you are happy to see them and that you are a friendly person, which makes you more interesting and attractive.

Expressing words of thanks is another key ingredient for building better and faster relationships. It can bring compatibility, make situations easier to deal with, and instill positive feelings in the person you are talking to.

Gratitude is a contagious thing. Give to the world and the world will give back to you. It is like a circle of happiness. Remember to say 'thank you' more often and show your gratitude through little actions. You can then make a difference not only in your life but also the life of those people around you.

The house of a thousand mirrors

Long time ago, there was a small, far away village with a place known as "The House of A Thousand Mirrors". One day, a little dog wandered into this extraordinary place and immediately found himself surrounded by a large number of other dogs. All of them looked as curious and excited as him.

The little dog then started wagging his tail. He raised his backside in the air and lowered his chest to the ground as an invitation to play with him. To his surprise, those dogs were doing the same. The little dog felt welcome and happy. He believed that this was the most wonderful place he had ever been.

Some time later came another dog that was quite older into this house. He carefully looked through the doorway and then saw many dogs staring at him. His ears lifted high and his whole body tensed up all of a sudden. He fixed his hard eyes at them and began to growl.

The other dogs were growling back at him right away which scared him so much that he quickly ran away from the house with his tail between his legs. As a result, he thought that this was the most awful place on the earth.

This is a Japanese folktale which has been told in two or more different versions, but they all convey the unique lesson; everybody around you is similar to the thousand mirrors, and how you see the outside world reflects what is inside you. Actually, the reflections you see in the faces of people you meet always give you some clues what kind of actions you have first taken towards them.

It is up to you whether you want to fill your life with positivity or negativity and get the same thing in return. However, if you find yourself getting irritated and frustrated easily even over little things, it may be an indication that you are being unhappy with something in your life.

Perhaps your job is draining you and you need to find another job or consider options for making the job work. Perhaps your personal finances are weakening and you need to get them in control. Perhaps your relationship begins to drift apart and it is time to make a few changes, put some effort into reconnecting, or even end it. Perhaps all that is needed is to see the life you are already living in a different way and you may not realize it.

When you are in a situation where you are not feeling good or when your mind is filled with so many thoughts and worries, being in a quiet place can calm your soul and help you rearrange your thoughts. Silence makes it easier to see what the true causes of your unhappiness are and what you really want to do with your life.

The key is for you to reflect on your own life — not look outside yourself for the answers. It can be astounding to discover that you have had the resources to deal with frustration and have been looking for them in all the wrong places.

Go to a park, a library, a specific cafe, an empty room, or somewhere that is free of noise and distractions. Then let your mind rest, recharge, and reorganize. Sort out your feelings like you are managing documents in filing cabinets.

When you can uncover your issues and realize that you are getting back on your path, you will feel confident and full of trust in yourself. As a result, annoying things and people do not bother you as much because only happy mind can lead you to see the good side of everything.

A ton of benefits of being a helper

Recently, I have had a chance to see a heartfelt dashcam footage recorded by a car that was waiting at a stop light. The two-minute video clip showed a group of pedestrians standing in the median between lanes of traffic with the sun above their heads. It was pretty chaotic on the streets as many drivers ignored pedestrians in crosswalks, and sometimes sped up or swerved to pass them.

However, these pedestrians soon finally made a lightning dash for the other side of the road -- except for one man. He clumsily placed one of his legs on the street before drawing it back as if he knew that he might not have been able to follow those people and make it across the rest of the way.

It was obvious that he had a problem with legs which had a harsh, painful impact on his walking speed. He ended up getting stuck by the raised curb facing with endless streams of cars until another group of pedestrians came up.

One of them was a woman with long straight red hair. From the camera angle, her face could not be seen but the way she dressed as well as her figure let me assume that she must be in her early twenties.

At first, she stood five feet away from the disabled man and patiently waited for a gap in traffic to come like other people. A moment later, she started to notice the man and slowly walked up to him. She would have asked him if he wanted her to help him cross the street because the man gladly nodded at her.

And that was how the video clip ended since the traffic light turned green and the driver needed to proceed. But he left a message under his own dashcam footage which has been uploaded on YouTube that, "I don't know who you are, but you're so beautiful to me."

In the meantime, there are a lot of people watching this video clip and expressing their positive opinions as well as admiration on her public act of kindness. Some men said that she was like an angel, and some hoped that they would find a girlfriend as thoughtful as her. Overall, a majority of viewers have wished her the best of luck in all of her future endeavors.

When you choose to help others, especially if it is face to face, you are making a positive impact not only on the people you are helping, but also on yourself.

Several studies have shown how helping other people can make you feel much happier as there is a link between better mental health and being a helper. It lowers rates of stress and depression while a warm feeling which results from knowing that what you have done selflessly means so much to someone else will boost your inner glow and make you look more gorgeous.

The Starting point of falling in love

When I was young, I liked to read Japanese manga, especially romantic ones. And almost every time the illustrators revealed the reason why two main characters of their stories had been falling in love with each other, it would frequently come from an impression that he or she was a nice person.

The hero or the heroine might accidentally see the other adopt an abandoned kitten, rescue a dog from drowning, or protect a weak child from bad people. This intrigued him or her even though they thought that the other was the most unpleasant person on the planet the first time they met.

Some men confess that a woman whom they used to consider dating with should have been beautiful, sexy, slender, and younger than them. That is what they had expected and they were able to actually meet that kind of woman in their real lives from time to time, only to find out later that things had never worked out between them.

They have jumped from one relationship to another until they found their current girlfriends whose qualities are fairly different from what these men have been looking for. She is an average woman who has nothing special, just some normal attributes. But she is empathetic, supportive, brave, honest, optimistic, and family oriented.

She usually radiates love and warmth from her heart that makes people around her feel happy. And the more time he has spent with her, the higher level of beauty he sees in her despite the fact that she has not made any changes on herself at all.

The more time passes by, the older you are, and the more people you meet, you will at last understand that what encourages us to stay in a long term relationship with someone, whether being a fiancé or a friend, is all about those good traits in the individual. The beautiful appearance of a person becomes worthless if he or she constantly conducts unwelcome behaviors. They are, as a result, being left alone because no one wants to get involved with them.

CHAPTER THREE
Positive actions develop relationships

Everyone's relationship is different and every relationship has its ups and downs - whether it is a short term or long term relationship, between parents and children, siblings, husband and wife, friends, coworkers, or manager and employee.

Conflicts are unavoidable when you have been in a relationship for more than a few days since your certain needs will go against one another's at some point and vice versa.

In fact, everybody has relationship problems. And sometimes you have them over and over and over. There are many issues and circumstances that can cause a relationship to falter or even stall, making you hurt, unhappy, and miserable most of the time. It is rare that relationship runs smoothly on the road without any bumps. Even a stranger can create a lot of tension and upset for the first time you meet him or her.

On a crisp spring day several years ago, I had been invited to participate in a charitable activity to provide food for people, especially the poor and the homeless. It was giving without conditions.

At our booth, there were many volunteers from various backgrounds and careers joining this meaningful event, and all of them were visibly ten year older than me.

The volunteer coordinator asked us to cook Thai food called "Som Tam" or spicy raw green papaya salad, one of Thailand's most popular dishes. The main ingredients consist of raw green papaya, garlic, tomatoes, bird's eye chilies, yard long beans, roasted peanuts, dried little shrimp which will be mixed together in a mortar and seasoned with palm sugar, lime juice, and fish sauce.

With its nutritional values, low calories, and full of flavor, it is usually considered to be one of Thai women's menus when they are on a diet. Also, Som Tam had been ranked sixth on "World's 50 best foods" which was compiled by CNN Travel in 2017. Steamed sticky rice, fresh vegetables, and grilled chicken are often eaten as side dishes to make it a perfect meal.

We were divided into three groups according to what duty we were assigned - preparing the ingredients, cooking, and serving. I was in a minor group that was responsible for assisting the cook in the preparation of the dishes which included peeling off the green skin of the raw papaya and grating or shredding it.

The bad news was that I had neither peeler nor knife - two important utensils for this task. I asked other volunteers in my group if any one of them appeared to have a spare one and then one woman in her upper 40s who sat across me burst out, "Didn't you prepare? Everyone here has taken their own tools from home."

The serious expression on her face and her verbal jabs stunned me for a moment. We had never met before so it was kind of strange to receive criticism from someone I barely knew. However, I did not argue back because seniority is given much importance in Thai society. It is always been a huge part of Asian culture to respect elders.

Moreover, I did not want to waste my time on defending myself since I knew well that we were not likely to change how someone else thought about us or how they delivered their opinion. The only thing I could really control was how I reacted to this situation.

Then I simply said sorry and went on finding a tool to start the work.

Few minutes later, I finally got a knife to peel the green papaya. However, it was not only getting the tools. It was actually knowing how to peel, chop and slice it into thin strips, and I unfortunately did not.

When other volunteers had finished grating two papayas, I was still struggling with chopping the first one in my hand and I started to feel a little embarrassed.

"How can you get it done by using a knife like that?"

The question came from the same woman who seemed to dislike me at first sight, and she sounded as annoyed as sarcastic this time. I could not help but wonder that complaining might be the only way she knew how to communicate.

However, her tone triggered anger in me as well. Yet, I chose to ignore her again, meanwhile, other volunteers showed me kindness by teaching me how to manually chop and shred a papaya with a knife until I was getting better and better at it.

During this time, we began to make small talk and someone in the group asked me my age as I looked way younger than all of them. It was not a big deal for a lot of Thai people to answer this kind of personal questions. It therefore turned into a little survey about age of the rest of us, and that irritable woman was no exception.

"Me? I'm really old. I'll turn 52 years old in the next few months." She said.

"Seriously? I can't tell you're that old." The words slipped out of my mouth before I could stop them. She stared me down.

"Why do you think so?" She carefully asked.

She did not look younger than her actual age. Her face was full of wrinkles whereas her skin became loose and flaccid. I did not think that praising her appearance was the best choice of answers, so I decided to give her a reply as honestly as I could.

"Well, it's because you still look spry, energetic, and healthy for me."

I said with a genuine smile. She looked at me for a moment and then nodded her head before quietly continuing to do her work. I thought that it would have been our last conversation.

At noon, we took turns to rest and grab something to eat. I was also hungry but hesitant to take a break. Suddenly, to my surprise, a plate of delicious food was placed on a table in front of me. I looked up to find who was so kind to serve me lunch.

"Let's eat while it's still hot."

It was her, and she was smiling at me.

The power of words

When you seriously consider what is the most powerful thing in the world that can inspire, motivate, and persuade; or discourage, dismiss, and dissuade you, you may find that ***words*** have that power.

In Japan, there is a belief that there are divine spirits which reside in words. It is known as 'kotodama', which is based on the idea of Shintoism, the traditional religion of Japan. The term literally means "the spirit of words" (koto = word, dama = spirit) and it is frequently mentioned in public discourse.

People who believe in *kotodama* think that names and words are alive and have special powers which can impact a person's life. Positive words are granted positive power; meanwhile, negative words will be given negative power by spirits.

Words are able to influence the way people think and the way they feel. As you can see from my story, a compliment sometimes can change people's mind and turn them into your friends. It should come as no surprise. Everybody likes to hear a good, well-natured compliment every now and then. It generates a good vibe which transmits efficiently between the one who offers those kind words and the one who receives them.

This concept also has been talked about in many self-help books. If you want to become successful, you have to beware of words you are using in your daily life.

Any words and thoughts can get stronger and sink into your subconscious mind by the repetitions which consequently have a long-lasting impact on your life. It is said that the different vibrations produced by different words would have effects ranging from inner peace, healing, protection, luck, and so forth.

There is this family consisting of grandparents and a teenage niece who is defiant, argumentative, and naughty. She did not put much effort into her class as well as her homework (if she did it) and, the worst of all, she liked to go out with friends and constantly arrived home late at night.

Her grandparents had tried everything they could think of but they were no further forward. No amount of begging, pleading, scolding, threatening, or yelling that could stop her inappropriate behaviors.

They found it very stressful and just did not know where to go next until they got an advice to not nag or criticize their niece but instead to pick up on all the little things she did well every day like doing the dishes or finishing her homework.

They followed advice without hesitation because they had nothing to lose. They started saying something nice about their niece's parents who got divorced for a while ago and kept mentioning all the good things they had ever done in the past when their niece was at home as often as possible.

It then appeared that their niece's behaviors have gradually changed in a better way. She stayed at home more often than before, paid more attention to her studies, and became more respectful. They, as a result, live happily together since then.

Misunderstandings, conflicts, and arguments in a family mostly result from poor communication between members. A recent study in Thailand seeks to explore what are the phrases that people hate to hear from their family.

The first one is "Go to hell." by 24%; the second one is offensive language by 19%; and the third one is "You should haven't been born as my child." by 16.5%.

It also shows the phrases that people want to hear from their family. The first one goes to "Are you tired?" by 20.2%; the second one is "I love you." by 16.1%; and the third one is "Do you need any help?" by 15.2%.

Asking your family members "How was your day?" or "Are you tired?" is a small thing that can make a big difference in your relationship. Because when you ask them these questions, you are indirectly telling them that they are seen, they are heard, and what they have done in order to support the family is recognized. It is the simplest way to show how much you care about them and how grateful you are for all hard work they do.

Let's admit it. We all hope that our family notices the good things we have done for them even if it is just a small success - the laundry is done, the cupboard is repaired, or the floor is cleaned. It is a beautiful feeling when we know that they notice our efforts and appreciate it.

As Carl Sandburg once said, "Be careful with your words, once they are said, they can only be forgiven, not forgotten." Regardless of whom you are talking to, think before you speak. Ask yourself, "Does your words offend or hurt another's feelings?" and learn to control your emotions.

Every time an aggressive thought rises up in your mind, be alert to that and pause for a moment and question its validity. Do not say anything that you do not want to hear from the others.

It is much easier to brush off something rude if a stranger says it. But when it comes straight from the mouth of the person you love, it cuts deep. It is not something you easily forget either.

It is a matter of patience

In reality, we have to deal with other people all the time. Wherever we are and whatever we do, there will be at least one person getting involved with us.

We always need to meet them, talk to them, and work with them. And the higher you go in an organization, the more people you are expected to interact with. That is when patience plays a key role.

To be successful in life, patience is needed daily. More than once, twice, or even a ton of times. You need to be able to endure not only hard work, but also unjustly criticism, blame, and insult. This is not something new but it is often overlooked.

Patience is represented as an important element of character around the world and for a long time ago. Kong Qiu, or Confucius, one of famous Chinese philosophers living during 551-479 bc said, "Patience is a close friend of intelligence." In every phase of human experience, we can see its need - in the workplace, on the road, and even at home.

You cannot hope to distance yourself from unpleasant situations, just as you cannot avoid interacting with someone you do not get along well with every once in a while. But if you possess this quality of patience and have long exercised it, you will finally go through every hardship with a result that you can be proud of.

Laura has met Nick at France when she was just twenty years old, whereas Nick was in his fifties. But their age gap was no barrier to romance as they were falling hard to each other. They believed that they were meant to be together and soon after that they made a decision to get married. Their parents gave their blessings but did not attend their wedding due to distance and several inconvenience issues.

Therefore, Laura was really nervous when Nick told her that he was bringing her to meet his parents for the first time. It was scary and intimidating because she wanted to be liked, and first impressions were very important. She came prepared.

She had learnt about some information on Nick's parents such as their beliefs, expectations, and interests beforehand in order that she could avoid doing anything to annoy them. She was also careful of what she was going to wear and her manners that might be considered disrespectful.

Everything seemed to be going well when Nick's parents welcomed her with smiles and they were having a wonderful dinner together.

But when two women were left alone in a living room afterwards, his mother then darkly asked Laura, "Can't you find any other man to be your husband? Why did you marry with someone as old as my son? Are you expecting to have access to his personal wealth?"

This created moments of shock for Laura. She instantly knew that she was having the biggest issue in her married life. Despite feeling hurt, Laura tried to politely explain how much she loved Nick and it had nothing to do with his money but her mother-in-law did not listen to her and insisted to not trust her.

It was really a hard time for Laura but giving up easily is not one of her traits. She tried to be helpful and nice to Nick's parents while she was spending few weeks at their house.

She took care of her mother-in-law the same way she did to her own mother. Nevertheless, she kept pushing

Laura away and introducing her as "a girlfriend" of her son to other people. Literally, she was particularly rude to her.

One year later, Laura gave birth to her daughter. During this time, she constantly called Nick's parents to keep in touch with them and to see if they needed anything. She wanted them to realize that she cared about them a whole lot, especially her mother-in-law.

She hoped to show her that she had no intention to take her son away from her and she was still a part of her son's life. However, her mother-in-law continuously bickered at her and disregarded her. Laura had no option but remained as strong and as enduring as possible.

It was not until Laura's daughter was three years old when Nick decided to visit his parents again. This time Laura resolved to be patient and respectful no matter how bad she was treated by her mother-in-law.

Certainly, the nasty comments started flying as soon as they met. But Laura just plastered a smile on her face, played deaf, and gave a warm reaction over her words and actions. In the meantime, she tried her best to take care of everyone in the family and improve herself if what her mother-in-law complained about her was true.

Just like constant dripping wears away the stone, Laura's persistence eventually won her mother-in-law's heart. She accepted her and perhaps grew to love her as she began to tell everyone that Laura was her daughter-in-law.

Laura's daughter was also one of main reasons to change her negativity. She was a little adorable girl who could make everyone around her laugh. Then unkind words and cold looks appeared to be gradually fading away. These days, Laura is very happy with her family life and harmony.

Every fumbles, obstacles, and setbacks require patience and repeated effort to overcome. If you can hang in there when it is hard to do so, no one and nothing can beat you.

You will manage to survive excellently when you face setbacks and failures. After all, you will be spiritually stronger and wiser. The more you can endure hardship and suffering, the better your life is. It will pay off in the long run.

A miracle of the lip balm pot

Long time ago, there was a woman who was married for few years with a man she thought to live the rest of her life with. The problem was, she recently found that her husband spent more time out than at home.

He would go to work early in the morning and came back very late at night. At first she was fine with that but sometimes he would come home after work and stay for a short period of time before going and visiting his friends. She saw his face again when it was around midnight.

She found herself getting irritated and upset, as they seemed to differ on what was a reasonable time for him to return home. As a result, they were often having the same fight over and over. She was feeling down and told her close friends about how dreadful her marriage life had become.

One of them suggested her to meet Mister A who seemed to have an ability to help others recover from illness and resolve miscellaneous problems. Some people even believed that he had a special power and many magical or miraculous "items" that could bring good luck and fortune to the holder.

After Mister A listened to her story, he took a lip balm pot out of his bag and handed it to her. He demanded that she apply this balm to her lips every morning and her husband would then stop socializing with everyone except her.

She should see this positive change within 2-3 months on one condition: she had to beware of whatever that was going to come out of her mouth. In other words, profanity and complaint were completely forbidden during using this lip balm. If it were otherwise, she would be unable to acquire the result she desired.

Sometimes life gets rough and we feel stuck without a real sense of how to take the next step forward even if we are desperate for a change. We start to look for advice or guidance and when we have the clue where to start, even the slightest one, we are ready to give it a try. The same goes for this woman. She had been feeling hopelessly trapped long enough, so she decided to do as Mister A told her.

That day, her husband came back home very late again and it made her really angry. She was going to yell at him but could stop herself just in time when she heard Mister A's voice in her head. *No curse. No complaint.*

The balm was already on her lips and it felt good. It left her lips nice and soft. She then tried to calm down and smiled at him when he walked in. She asked him what he wanted to drink or eat and followed through. And when he got prepared to go outside, she walked up to the door with him and told him to drive safely.

Overall, she tried to be the coolest wife in the world even though she was far from it. However, the unbelievable thing happened after two months passed by.

Her husband would head home at the end of a workday, quietly rest at his favorite chair while she was cooking, and then they had dinner together. His nights out became less and less frequent.

She was fascinated by this change of his behaviors and almost thought that it was the magic of the lip balm, but not before her husband put all his cards on the table and told the entire story of what was going on. And it had nothing to do with the lip balm.

He confessed to her that he used to be as uncomfortable as restless when he had been staying at home, and she was a major reason to make him feel that way.

It was incredibly boring and unbearable for him as he had to listen to her endless complaint every time he came home after a long day at work. It just made him more tired.

That was why he tried to avoid being at home. But since she quit complaining and started giving him kind words and sweet smiles lately, he found home a place of peace and joy once again.

A dirty laundry

A newly married young couple moved into a new neighborhood.

The next morning while they were eating breakfast, the wife looked out the window and noticed that her neighbor was hanging different items of clothes on the clothesline.

"Oh, dear. They're all still dirty." She remarked, "I doubt what detergent she use or she might haven't known how washing should be done properly."

The husband followed her gaze, but said nothing.

A week later her neighbor hung her laundry out to dry again and the wife could not help complaining about its dirt with her husband who listened to her but made no comment.

One day, the wife looked out the window and, to her surprise, she saw a nice clean wash on her neighbor's clothesline.

"Look, honey. Her laundry finally comes out clean now." She exclaimed before turning her head to look at her husband who was reading a newspaper at the kitchen table, "Did you tell her about it?" She wondered.

"No, I've said nothing to her." the husband replied calmly. "I got up early this morning and just cleaned our windows."

Half a watermelon

It was a very hot and humid summer day and David just finished his work. He went straight home, hoping to get some cool drinks and take a shower as soon as possible.

The first thing he did after being home was to go to the kitchen and open a refrigerator. He then found a cut watermelon half wrapped tightly with plastic wrap. Gladly, he took it out and ate it all.

Thirty minutes later, his wife, Silvia, came back home, carrying multiple grocery bags in her hands.

"It's so hot out there! I'm very thirsty." She said before opening the fridge. "Huh? Where's the watermelon?" She blurt out.

David told her that he already ate it and noticed a gloomy expression on his wife's face, but she did not say anything. Silvia then took a bottle of water out of fridge, only to find it empty.

She frowned at him. "What are you doing? You came home first, didn't you? Why don't you pour water into a bottle?"

Her questions instantly upset him. "Do I need to do every task in this house?" David retorted.

As a result, they did not talk for a week.

On Saturday, David decided to go visit his parents who lived not far from him alone. When his parents saw him, they immediately looked for Silvia and their children. David had no choice but tell them about the argument between him and his wife.

"It's just half a watermelon. Why did she have to make such a big deal about it?" David said after his mother chided him for not keeping some watermelon for Silvia.

His father let out a chuckle. "I see. Well, it's Sunday tomorrow. You'd better bring your wife and kids here. I want to meet them and we'll have dinner together."

Next day, David and his family went to see his parents and spend their time over there altogether. Few hours before dinner, his father asked him to go to the local grocery store and buy some spices like cinnamon, thyme, and garlic powder that happened to get used up fast in his parent's house. When he came back, he was informed that Silvia was taking kids on a walk.

"You're sweating like a pig." His father remarked before brining half a watermelon out of fridge and handing it with a spoon to David. "Have some. It can quench your thirst."

"Wow." David exclaimed while holding the half of watermelon in his hands, "Where did you get it? I've never seen a watermelon as big as this one. This half must be not less than 3 pound weight."

"Share it with your wife then if you think you can't eat it all." His father said.

David nodded and took a spoonful of watermelon. It was juicy and sweet which helped his body cool down. As he predicted, he could not eat the whole half cut watermelon so he stored the rest of watermelon in the refrigerator.

After dinner, David was summoned to his father's study. Then his father showed him two pieces of half cut watermelon and asked him, "Can you tell me the difference between them?"

Despite being confused, David looked down to consider watermelon. One half was eaten by him and the other half was also eaten.

"I don't see any difference." He replied.

His father stared at him in silence for a while before pointing at the watermelon. "You ate this half and Silvia ate this half." He explained. "I told both of you to share it with one another if you couldn't eat it all. Now look at how your wife used her spoon. She only ate half side of the watermelon and obviously didn't touch its other side. Then look at yours. You only ate the center of the watermelon where the good stuff is at and left the rest for your wife. But we all know that the delicious part of the watermelon is the pink flesh, don't we?"

David immediately felt embarrassed and appeared at a loss for words.

"Do you know where love is between couples?" His father asked and continued without waiting for David's answer. "It's in a cup of soup, a loaf of bread, and even a jug of water. This seems to be little things but they can impact your life in profound ways. Let's think about it. If Silvia had gone back home before you, she would have kept that watermelon for you like the way she did today. On the other hand, how would you feel if your wife always acts thoughtlessly and inconsiderately like you? Could you be happy with that?"

With his father's guidance, David could see the other side of the story much more clearly. This time he got into a fight with his wife and tried to make excuses even though he was at fault. An uncomfortable slide of guilt abruptly ran down David's stomach. He resolved to improve himself and treat his wife more nicely from then on.

Think the other way round

You have already read three interesting stories: A miracle of the lip balm pot, A dirty laundry, and Half a watermelon. And you might notice some significant issues.

You can see the miserable, angry, bitter woman who wanted her husband to spend more time with her and took time to realize that it was her part in pushing him away, the woman who believed that her neighbor did not know how to do laundry and never thought that it was her own windows which were not clean, and David who was so preoccupied with himself and his needs that he forgot to appreciate the small things that his wife had regularly done for him.

The situations are different but they all do convey one lesson; do not be too quick to judge others, especially if your perspective of life is clouded by anger, jealousy, negativity or unfulfilled desires.

It is easy for us to point at others and criticize their shortcomings, flaws or wrong doings. It is convenient for us to point at each other and blame one another for our personal pain and disappointments. The truth is, however, when you point a finger at someone, there are three pointing back at you.

This is just a reminder for you to stop blaming others and take responsibility for your current situations and feelings instead. Think about it. Are you treating others nice enough before you criticize or judge them?

Looks and good appearances can be an open door to love, but habits and behaviors will play a key role to determine whether a couple can keep their relationship strong and healthy, and even make love last.

The biggest single obstacle to maintaining healthy relationship is "self-deception," where you believe yourself to be right whereas your partner to be wrong. And even if you know that you are - mainly or partly - at fault, you make an attempt to excuse your behaviors or actions by creating an explanation that *sounds good*.

Making excuses and complaining about how unfair life is cannot solve your problems and sometimes just make things worse. Sadly, people will continue to make them until they realize that excuses are just that excuses.

In order to secure a solid foundation in your relationship, it is important to look closely at your behaviors and get rid of those which can be harmful to your loving relationship.

When one another hurt you in some ways, it is time for you to think over a problem thoroughly and look back at yourself first because we are quick to see other people's faults, but are blind to our own ones. In spite of this knowledge, we seem to make the same mistake over and over again.

But when you are able to interrupt these patterns and actively engage in healthier ways of interacting with your partner, you feel more closeness and contentment. On the other hand, without this approach, you inevitably find both of you growing apart over time.

Do not measure others with your ruler

You are probably looking for a serious relationship and someone who is young, single, well educated, and fun-loving, with a good shape physically. This may be the essential qualities that you find indispensable in your future partner would have to be. But we all have both positive and negative personality traits. After all everyone has flaws or shortcomings.

If you want to live your life happily, you need to accept difference in others - whether it is race, religion, ethnicity, sexual preference, social status, attitude, belief, culture, hobby and whatsoever. In fact, differences are what make the world interesting.

No two people are the same even though they are raised under the same environment and conditions. We are growing up with our own story and past. Each experience in life brings about understanding and perspective. And perspective is what makes people unique.

Ordering food and drinks is the most obvious example of it. I like to eat a green papaya salad or "Som Tam" once in a while and it will literally taste so delicious when it contains a lot of spices.

However, I have the low tolerance to spicy food so every time I ordered a papaya salad, I told a cook that I did not want it too spicy. Still, I often got a papaya salad that was way too spicy for me.

Why? It is because a level of spiciness of the cook is different from mine. Therefore, she would find that a papaya salad with six chili peppers is not spicy, whereas two chili peppers can make me break out in an uncontrollable sweat.

Then I have learned that I should change the way I order my papaya salad. Instead of telling the cook that I do not want it too spicy, I should indicate how many chili peppers I want to add in my dish. With this, I could make the cook have the same viewpoint as I have.

We know that nobody is perfect, but it is more complex than that because traits which are considered negative may depend on the observer.

Some negative traits are obviously negative in everyone's eyes, while the negativity of other traits can depend on the eye of the beholder. Someone who is generally considered as a very kind and helpful person may turn to be a 'too nice' or 'too annoying' person for someone else. Positives become negatives this way, depending on who is doing the observation.

You may already have found several negative traits in others. You may even have shared your opinion and expected that person to work on that negative trait.

Everyone, however, has some bad traits in personality, and yes, including you. And it is quite likely that you do not realize how it appears to others or even find it your fault. Reverse the situation. What if someone were judging you and not accepting you? How would you feel? Keep these questions in mind the next time you are criticizing other people.

It is very tempting to see the world in black and white with a right and wrong way to do things, but that is not how it is. Things do not have to be right or wrong if you stop labeling your way as 'right'.

Many people have a misconception that they are superior to others in intelligence or ability, resulting them to think that other people should follow their codes and principles of conduct.

An attempt to get others to follow their way is based on the thought that they are correct while others are wrong. And this is the main reason why we can find fault in other people or things easier than we can find faults in ourselves. It is because the self is the beginning point of reference by which we judge anything else.

It is so easy to abstractly think of ourselves as a nice, open-minded and accepting person. Anything we perceive is normal to us which makes most of us terrible at introspection.

In the meantime, the idea of attempting to change others is wrong and impractical. No one can change other people if they do not feel to change it themselves. Actually, we ourselves prefer to cling to the habitual behavior, so it is the same with others. And such judgment and lack of acceptance will jeopardize the healthy relationships.

Although you cannot change someone's negative personality traits, your good manners can impress, inspire, and influence them. If they appreciate your manners, they would change themselves by having you as their model.

But if they show no interest in changing, do not waste your time to make a complaint. Try to work on paying more attention to your thoughts instead and do your best to push them in a non-judgmental direction. Remember that accepting things as they are and let go of what you cannot control is the key to true happiness.

Release your expectations

If you take an observation of the life of people around you as well as of your own, you will find that the longer we stay with someone, the more easily we tend to lose our temper on them.

The reason is that we have expected too much from them. We want their ways of talking or thinking to be no different from ours. We always hope that they would pay a respect to our feelings and act according to our needs, but frequently end up with considerable stress and disappointment instead. This is a usual mistake that can be found in most relationships.

Certainly, it is reasonable to expect your partner to have a greater interest in you than the average person. You deserve basic things in relationships, like honest and respect. But by counting on anything other than that you are putting yourself through unnecessary suffering in life.

Having overly high desires only makes you chronically unhappy because your partner will never be able to fulfill your expectations.

When it comes to relationships, it is important for you to consistently look for the good in your partner rather than the bad. When he or she gives you a really hard time, you may stop for a moment and look at things from his or her perspective.

Every person on this earth has a problem of his own but he may refuse to let others know. He would wear a mask that always smiles to hide his pain and fear. In fact, most of people find it hard to reveal their true feelings when they have a tough upbringing.

Considering what they are really going through and how they feel are, therefore, the key concept in becoming understanding which leads to empathy and forgiveness. Allow people to make mistakes and learn from them. Accordingly, you will not try to offend them for what they have done or hurt them with an insult which usually makes things worse.

Positive thoughts always lead to positive words and positive actions. A great attitude is beneficial for every aspect of your life. It can help you to improve your mood, work productivity, relationship, and so forth.

When you think that you are being with a great man (or woman), the way you talk and treat towards him or her are likely to change, in a good way. You will be more respectful, grateful, and considerate. Chances are your relationship will be getting better.

Remember that everyone is at a different place on their journey, so their words and actions will reflect that. And it is completely normal if your partner has a different opinion from you. Nobody is bound to agree with every word you say.

Actually, the only person you should set expectations for is yourself. If you find yourself focusing on what is wrong in your life, what you do not have, or what you are missing out on, adjust your attitude by choosing to think differently.

When you accept difference and imperfection, you will not ever feel sad, upset, and disappointed again. You begin to feel, day by day, barely noticing it, that something wonderful has taken hold of your life again. It is happiness.

It does not matter how big your house is; it is how lovely the laugh that fills within your home. It is not what car you have; it is how safely you can drive home. It is not how many connections you make; it is people who stay by your side and say, "Everything will be all right. You still have me here." when you are experiencing difficult life challenges.

CHAPTER FOUR
Positive actions lead to success.

When it comes to luck, whether bad or good, we often think of an unpredictable phenomenon or things that happen in our lives merely through chance. None of us are lucky all of the time and yet, there are some people who tend to be luckier than others.

In fact, lucky people are not lucky by sheer accident. They are lucky because they prepare themselves to welcome luck. They understand that they are unable to control the weather, the company's policy or the economy. They also do not let bad luck stop them from trying to create their own good fortune.

As you may have heard, good luck is something that we can create by hard work and optimism. Dr. Richard Wiseman, a professor at the University of Hertfordshire, has confirmed this saying by spending many years examining the behaviors of lucky and unlucky individuals.

In his one of best-selling psychology books, *The Luck Factor,* he has described that only the 10 percent of charmed lives is truly random. The remaining 90 percent is a state of mind—a way of thinking and behaving.

People with a lot of stress, hope, and hype often put blinders on and miss to notice chance opportunities, whereas lucky people adopt a relaxed attitude and shape their interactions with others in a positive way. They are also aware of what is going on in their situation, which opens them up to opportunities that exist right in front of them.

The tale of a lucky man

Everybody who knew William said that he was really lucky after he had been hired to renovate a school kitchen and received tens of thousands of dollars in return, without making any bid presentations to compete against other candidates.

They all wondered why he got this job very easily, and would be surprised if they found that what he did was just show kindness towards strangers few months ago.

William is the father of two children living in Malaysia. He is a full time architect and works part time as a property manager.

It all started one Saturday afternoon when he was buying some household products as a grocery store in town. A couple who looked like tourists stepped in and asked a cashier for directions to a museum. William knew this museum very well because it was located near his house.

He, therefore, turned his face to the couple and explained the direction to them. The female tourist then asked him about an estimate taxi fare to get there. After receiving a reply from William, she started talking to the man who came with her in their own language.

It was a fairly far distance from where they were to the museum, so William asked if he could give them a lift to their destination since it was on his way back home anyway. The couple appreciated his offer.

Along the way, William tried his best to introduce about his hometown - the places that the couple should visit and the things they did not want to miss. As William drove past a local market which was open every weekend, he then told the couple that he would go there the next day, so they could come and meet him if they wanted to.

It was a vague invitation but, to his surprise, William really found the couple at the market on the next morning. Then they spent time talking, shopping, and dining together.

When William knew that the couple had recently formed a private school and were looking for decorating ideas, he took both of them to see many parts of the building which he had operated in partnership with others in order to help them to find inspiration.

What William did was just an act of kindness. But it turned out that the couple was very impressed by the kitchen design which was his own creativity and then they offered him a project. This was an unexpected opportunity he had received from other people, not to mention to the fact that they knew each other only for two days.

When you interact with others, be sure your behaviors and actions are as positive as possible. Showing courtesy and kindness without concern for reward will allow you to build healthy relationships in a long run. When you treat people well, they will be willing to work for you, buy from you, and help you to achieve your goals and dreams.

There is a general conception that if you want to make a good impression and establish a certain level of trust with your Spanish counterparts, it is advisable to be friendly and approachable. Spaniards prefer to develop a personal relationship and build social bonds before starting business discussions.

Therefore, a first meeting in Spain tends to be relaxed and informal. It will normally begin with talking from general matters to more specific issues, such as the cuisine, customs, sports, and family life.

Honesty and likeability play an integral part in successful negotiations in Spain. You may have heard the quote, "People do business with people they know, like and trust." This is a fundamental rule of business and you could find it true in most cases.

I was once looking for a new table for my living room, so I went to one of famous home furnishing stores which was very far from my home. There, I found the product that I really liked and wanted to buy. It was beautifully designed and its size was perfect. The price was reasonable too. I really thought - I'm going to buy this.

I walked up to a store staff to get more details about it, but he only spoke to me if I was asking him a question. He neither smiled nor provided any further useful information to me. A poor customer treatment made me think twice to make a purchase. Finally, I went out of the store without spending any money.

The following week, I went to another store and bought a table with less beautiful design and color options. But I felt I was welcome as the staff over there was willing to listen to me and patiently helped me to choose products.

The quality of product is important, but if a brand fails to make a good connection with prospective buyers, countless potential sales will be lost. After all, entrepreneurs who can treat their customers like family, not strangers, are likely to be as influential and successful as they would like.

A fish that can be eaten throughout the year

Long time ago, there was a millionaire who were looking for a good man to marry his only one daughter. He had made a decision that his future son-in-law must be wise, intelligent, and virtuous enough to take care of household assets and his daughter.

To find that ideal man, the millionaire set up a puzzle and every man who wanted to become a member of his family needed to solve it. The question was: "If you have caught one fish from a lake, what would you do with it so that you can eat it throughout the year?

Everyday a large number of men walked to the millionaire's house with their answers. They suggested breeding or preserving fish by using various methods such as dehydrating, salt curing, and so on.

But none of these answers could satisfy the millionaire, not until a young fine man appeared and said, "I think I'm trying to cook fish soup and then fill the bowls before distributing them to all my relatives and neighbors. With this, I'll have the food to eat throughout the year because when my relatives or neighbors cook something, they would share it with me as well."

As soon as the millionaire heard this answer, a big smile crossed his face. He gave his consent and approval to this young man to marry his daughter at last.

Sharing has the power to get you close to other people and deepen all of your relationships. A fool does not like to share with others because he fears of inadequacy. He thinks that sharing will reduce what he has and then he will become insufficient and insecure. But a wise man knows that sharing will allow him to get more.

One obvious example of this is knowledge sharing. The more often you teach others what you know, the more proficient and smarter at that area you will become.

Giving others equals giving yourself, and it does not mean only money or things. It can be labor, love, ideas, experiences, time, and opportunities. Make a decision to give wherever you go, to whomever you see. As long as you are giving, you will be receiving.

Sincerity is the best source of trust

No matter what job you are doing, you will be assigned important tasks, put in a good position when it comes time for a promotion or happy with a big order from a client if you can get people whom you are working or negotiating with to trust you.

Contrarily, if your conduct is misleading or deceptive, or likely to mislead or deceive, you may be able to make a lot of money from selling your products or services but it would only happen for a short period of time. Sooner or later people will detect your lies and then refuse to work with you or buy from you again. Additionally, you would be charged with this offense.

Trust is worth gold whether in business, friendship or family. It takes time to build trust. In other words, gaining trust requires effort and patience. And it can run deep as long as you do the right things.

Unfortunately, it can be broken in a split second if you fail to prove as a person who can be reliable. And when you lose it, it is very difficult - if not possible - to rebuild it.

In a business environment, establishing trust is very essential. It is a greater determinant of success than anything else. The more trust people have in you, the easier it is to grow and nurture your business.

One of the most imperative traits to build trust is sincerity. It can be a tremendous asset to you as a leader in an organization. Many successful people are always honest with their customers, coworkers, and employees which in turn brings trust and loyalty to them.

Building trust is about showing people that you are honest to them and mostly care about their benefits, not yours. You have to introduce the value of your products and services with clarity, regularly share information, always deliver on what you have promised, and instantly address a damage to them directly when you make a mistake.

A sincere person is much more apt to admit he or she is wrong, and other people appreciate that honesty. What instils credibility and reliability is frequently as a result of how you deal with concerns and problems. This is a reason why a person who is sincere easily develops trust with people around him. He or she keeps telling the truth and being honest even in admitting weakness or vulnerability.

Certainly, people can fake what they say and how they act with others. In fact, some people are really good at it. How to identify good and bad people is not an easy task. But if you are not too ignorant and spend time to look close enough, you will notice the signs that help you to discover their values.

The outside does not always reflect the state of a person's mind but his actions, words, and expressions may give some clues on what his true personality is. See how he interacts with his family and others, especially people below his social status. Does he help others without seeking recognition? Or is it all about himself? Look at how he spends his time and money will give insights into his inner self.

Sincerity is not something you can completely fake, and it is wiser to not claim to be something you are not or pretend to know more than you do. You cannot just go through the motions because people can sense whether you want to genuinely be friends with them and support each other or not. When you encounter someone who is truly sincere, he or she exudes a genuineness that is undeniable. You can feel it not only through face-to-face communication but also telephone and email.

A friend of mine once worked as a customer service representative in a company that sells auto parts around the world. At that time, the company was trying to convince one of potential clients in Africa to try out the product. They expected this valued part of a business strategy to give them a chance to open new market and receive a purchase order. But things were not that rosy.

The problem was that the prospective company in Africa refused to accept the product samples which had been sent via a courier because there was an additional shipping cost. It was nearly $100 and the recipient had to pay it so that the package could be delivered.

The supervisor of my friend had sent email to this company several times trying to explain the situation as well as ask them to pay the charge without forgetting to let them know that they would get paid back. However, they responded to his email with a vague answer and evaded the request.

Then my friend was assigned to deal with this future client. She spent one month before successfully convincing them to accept the samples with additional shipping cost. Her supervisor was really happy and impressed by her work.

She told me that what she did was only to rewrite her supervisor's email messages. In contrast with her supervisor who seemed to use a lot of sophisticated vocabularies in his email, she chose to use simple words and sentences that were able to carry meaning the way she wanted.

She also assured them that her company repaid them the money that they paid in advance. The thing was, she had not the slightest doubt if her company would pay off this debt. Then she unconsciously and honestly conveyed this trust while she was writing the email. They were delivered to this client at last.

Actually, the problem of this case is not the amount of money that was required to pay, but it is all about trust. As Stephen R. Covey, a businessman and the author of the best-selling book, "The Seven Habits of Highly Effective People" once said, "When the trust account is high, communication is easy, instant, and effective."

It can be really difficult to sell if your customers do not believe in you and your product. Trust is not a matter of technique, tricks, or tools but of character. We are trusted because of our way of being, not because of our polished exteriors or our expertly crafted communications.

The sheer passion and dedication can make you shine

Haneda International Airport is one of the two major airports in Japan and serves approximately 200,000 passengers every day. Anyone who visits here would be amazed and impressed by shiny polished floors, dust-free windows, and fresh-smelling bathrooms.

Actually, Haneda Airport was presented with first place in the 2018 "World's Cleanest Airport" category. This is the third year in a row that it has received this award voted by air travelers, according to Skytrax, an aviation service research firm based in United Kingdom.

This extraordinary achievement has been largely credited to Niitsu Haruko who has spent over twenty years focusing on her cleaning job in Haneda Airport and was lately honored as a national treasure craftsman.

Every morning she chooses walking up a 50-step staircase over an escalator in the subway station and shows up at the airport very early. After that, she lifts five kilogram dumbbells for around twenty minutes in order to exercise the muscle groups in her stomach and arms before starting her work.

"Cleaning is a job that requires a lot of strength. I need to maintain good health." She said.

She begins her first task of the day with patrolling the area surrounding Haneda Airport to detect dirt, dust, and a stain regardless of how tiny they can be. She checks all over the place - whether it is behind a television, under a chair, a handrail, an automatic door, a baggage cart, a toilet seat cover, inside a toilet rim, and so forth. If there is a blot, regardless of how small it is, she will stop to clean it up without any delay.

Niitsu can explain the specific use of over 80 cleaning products and analyze within minutes the cause and compositions of each stain as well as what kind of equipment to use to remove that spot. In fact, many cleaning tools are made by her so that she can wipe off dirt every corner and crevice of the airport.

As simple as her task may seem, Niitsu never compromises on quality of her work. For example, when it comes to cleaning a toilet, she not only wipes a countertop, scrubs a sink, washes a toilet bowl, and mops a floor, but she also cleans a hand dryer because it can cause an odor after it has been used several times while the air inside the restroom are not circulating properly.

In the meantime, she avoids using irritant chemicals that will affect guests. She thoroughly cleans difficult-to-reach spots and floors to remove all traces of dust because many people, especially children who do not have immune systems as efficient as adult, can suffer an allergic reaction when exposed to dust.

Niitsu is a middle-aged woman born in Shenyang, the capital of China's northeast Liaoning Province. Her family relocated to Japan when she was 17 years old. At that time, she could barely speak Japanese and was the target of bullying in school because of her mixed heritage.

Due to the language barrier, the only job she thought that she was capable of doing was cleaning. She then started her first part-time cleaning job since high school and has been accepted to work as a cleaner at Haneda Airport when she was twenty three years old.

There, she met her manager Suzuki Mazaru who was an expert of cleaning in the airport. He inspired her to enjoy doing her cleaning job and to push herself in her career. Niitsu tried very hard to improve her skills of cleaning in order to make him appreciate her work.

However, three years passed by and he never gave her any compliments, not before she learned that cleaning is not only about techniques or skills but also the understanding of emotional connection with guests.

After that, she won a National Building Cleaning Competition and Suzuki Mazaru came to congratulate her for the effort made and the important result achieved. It made her really glad that her manager finally noticed and admired her work.

Niitsu is now working in a managerial position leading a cleaning team at the airport which consists of approximately 700 people. And her presence was known to the mass in Japan after being featured in an NHK documentary about a professional craftsman.

Many people have visited her at the airport just to express their gratitude for all her excellent work. She also has been invited to share her knowledge about cleaning at a particular company or organization and on many TV programs. In addition, she has published a best-selling book telling about her life and teaching people how to efficiently clean their houses.

While Niitsu always works far beyond simple cleaning because she loves her job and regards it as an artisan, a lot of people do not take the cleanliness as well as their job for granted.

They work just to earn money, bonus, fame or prize. I do not say they should not. Actually, there is not something wrong with that. But only thinking of what you can gain from doing something is not potential enough to produce a great work and impress people.

If you want to be remarkable in your work, you need to be willing to put yourself completely into it and focus on the needs of others before your own.

Emotional engagement is worth the investment

When it comes to business, caring and sharing the feelings of others are also a kind of investment. When you are giving someone a piece of your heart - whether it is a small contribution like kind words and attentiveness or a large contribution like money and gifts - you are developing or deepening a bond with that person which can bring a different kind of reward now and in the future.

Den Fujita, a wealthy Japanese founder of McDonald's Japan, has once mentioned in his book that he has found that emotional engagement is a worthwhile investment that qualifies as high return and low risk.

Every year, he pays a large amount of money to the hospital as a fund for reserving its beds. When his employees or their family members have an illness or an accident, they will receive immediate medical treatment.

Additionally, he has also established a wonderful idea that the staff's birthday is an individual holiday. They do not need to come to work. They can freely and happily arrange their time to celebrate and take a rest.

Mr. Fujita believes that when an employee is engaged, they go above and beyond their normal duty. They will be more productive and motivated in their work which leads to higher profits for an organization.

Treating employees as individuals and looking for ways to foster solid relationships is one of the most important factors in determining how successful a company can become. In fact, there are tons of examples of companies that have achieved massive success because of how they treat their employees.

Emotions are a huge part of the customer experience as well. How you respond when an individual comes to you with a need or a problem can trigger different customer's behavior which also impacts customer loyalty and retention. While caring can be a means of coming up with an appreciation of the other, lacking of empathy can lead to a less favorable outcome.

In the past decade, to understand why some physicians were sued far more than others, researchers started analyzing audio recordings between 124 doctors and at least 10 of their patients.

A study has found that the way doctors communicate with patients appeared to increase or decrease the chances of a malpractice suit.

Doctors who spent time listening intently to a patient's situation in a manner that was non-judgmental and open fully to the patient's perspective before a definitive action was undertaken were less likely to be sued than doctors who just looked at his notepad most of the time during investigation and usually made patient feel rushed or ignored. In other words, poor communication was one of the most significant predictors of filing a claim of a patient.

Doctors who were not sued did medical errors or make a mistake too but they were forgiven by patients because they could make patients have affection for them. They tended to give more medical information and be more willing to explain treatment options, side effects, and associated risks to patients. They were also much more likely to have a good sense of humor, to display empathy, and to encourage patients to talk and to ask questions during their visits.

In this sense, lawsuits are not random. Good communication between doctors and patients can enhance patients' satisfaction and affection which resulting in helping doctors to avoid being sued.

Patients prefer a feeling of connectedness with their doctors who they can share their opinions and concerns. On the other hand, when patients feel a lack of respect and compassion, it increases the likelihood of an avoidable adverse outcome.

Generally, people respond better to more genuine-feeling and nurturing interactions. When you invest in providing the very best service to each of your customers and make them feel good, respected, and important, you are prompting them to reciprocate with an open mind and loyalty which make it much easier for them to return to you as well as to recommend your services to others in their network.

You will also gain their gratitude and trust. And the more gratitude they feel, the more they will like you. The more they like you and feel comfortable with you, the more you are capable of changing their minds and getting them to act in desired ways.

Goodwill brings good future

Everyone knows that the present time is the most important time of our lives while the events from yesterday no longer exist and the future has yet to unfold. We cannot predict what is going to happen and what we will encounter in the future - even tomorrow or the next hour or the next minute. As Forrest Gump played by Tom Hanks in the movie by the same name said, "Life is like a box of chocolates. You never know what you're gonna get."

Focusing on living in the now and choosing to do good at every opportunity, therefore, would be the only way that can help guarantee a better, brighter, and more successful future.

Amy has worked as a librarian in a law firm. One day she received an email from a fee earner who had left the firm for a while to join a telecommunication company as an in-house lawyer.

In his email, he asked her to help him to get a draft Act which would be likely to affect the telecommunications industry if it was passed and approved by Parliament.

Amy was really surprised by his request because he barely spoke to her unless it was about work when they were still in the same company. They were neither close nor distant and they were not friends. Nevertheless, she quickly searched for what he wanted and sent it to him as soon as she found it.

He thanked her and Amy had not heard from him since then. She thought they would not see each other, speak, or email anymore.

But after two years has passed, the company that Amy has worked for wanted this ex-fee earner to return to his old position because they have had an enormous amount of impression and trust in his abilities and intelligence, so they approached him with a job offer.

He accepted it and started to work in the same place as Amy once more. Shortly afterwards he has been promoted to partnership with the firm.

Amy does not know whether he can remember the last time she did him a favor or not, and she is not the type of person who expects something in return from helping others anyway. However, there are many signs that he has tried to support her career progression since he becomes a partner.

He has also made his own suggestions and provided feedback on areas where Amy can develop in order that she can enhance chances of getting a higher role in the company.

Things would be different if Amy thought that this man was just a cold person who only talked to her when he needed something and then ignored to help him. As you see, the future is uncertain and changeable. You might not want to work with your ex-line manager or other colleagues again, but paths might cross with them in an unexpected way in the future.

Truth is, the type of success that you achieve in life is largely determined by how much people like and respect you. A well-developed social circle will help you retain respect, credibility, and likability. However, a good relationship does not just happen - you have to work at it. And effective personalities play a key role in gaining success.

Personality characteristics are based on consistent patterns of thought and behavior you have accumulated throughout the course of your life. It is something that makes a person unique. The good news is that it is learnable and trainable to have personality traits that are characteristic of successful people.

No matter what kind of person you have been in the past, or how much you have tended to get caught up in negative habits, you can change. Through repetition and practice, you can shape your character traits in a better way and become one of the most efficient as well as attractive people, which leads you to success in the future.

Epilogue

Along life's journey, we all encounter three basic types of people. Firstly, it is the supporter. This person could manifest in a variety of forms such as a family member, teacher at school, life coach, or friend. They will encourage your personal growth, inspire you to get up and get moving, and guide you on the path to success.

Secondly, it is acquaintance. They appear to be dispassionate about the things that happen around you. They would not completely ignore you but they neither support nor hinder you. You have likely met them rather than other two types of people because almost everyone is busy enough with his or her own life problems. The last one is the enemy. This person not only dislikes you but also stands in your way of achieving your goals.

Successful people tend to have a strong support network. They realize that it is impossible to work alone or in a vacuum. They then focus on what they can offer and use their talents in ways that help others in order to make new friends and connections.

The reality is that you need others to more or less help you grow and open doors of opportunity for you when you are pursuing your dreams. Without these people in your corner, it is really difficult to create the success you want to reach.

Fortunately, you can build this powerful network as well as turn your acquaintance and enemies into your supporters - and it all starts with *a thought*.

Believe it or not, your actions always reflect your thought and mind. When you find someone irritating, annoying and off-putting, whether because of how they behave or what they have done to you, you may not actually treat them with rudeness but you may have a tendency to frown and rarely smile when you are interacting with them.

These small actions you take will in turn create negative feelings toward you and inevitably bring about an enemy. Such people can be a very powerful force and make you slow down or even stop moving towards your goals.

Having a lot of ill-wishers in life will feel like you are sailing in heavy weather with high winds and waves which makes it harder and more exhausting to reach a destination than when you are sailing in calm weather.

On the contrary, if you choose to be a positive thinker, you are going to say and do nice things even when something goes wrong. Actually, the nature of every situation is just measured by your perspective.

If your boss gives you more work to do while your colleagues play on the internet all day long, instead of giving in to frustration, first look at the good side.

You are selected because your boss possibly trusts in the capabilities and qualities you possess. He or she may want to test you before bringing you to a better role in the team. Above of all, you will surely gain a precious experience from doing that task.

With this attitude, you will show more willingness to accept extra work and assignments - which leads to admiration and appreciation. And the support will come to you at last.

When you look at a tree, you can see its trunk, branches, and leaves. You will as well spot its flowers or fruits during spring time or harvest season. But the most important part of a tree is its root which, in most cases, is invisible to the eye since it is beneath the ground.

Truth is, a tree's canopy and root system are linked. A strong root leads to a healthy and stable tree as an old saying goes, "The deeper the roots, the higher the branches." If you plant a tree and want it to grow big and broad, you need to take a good care of its root. Similarly, if you want happiness and success in your life, you need to have healthy roots.

Having healthy roots is having positive thoughts. Both of them do not seem so obvious, but they are like the foundation of a building. As Oprah Winfrey once said, "If you want your life to be more rewarding, you have to change the way you think."

You will become successful when you are honest, diligent, considerate, and patient enough. And these wonderful qualities cannot come from bad attitudes. It may sound cliché, but it is really true.

If you do not know where to start, simply attempt to approach others with more kindness and understanding because positive actions can lead to positive thinking. Think of it this way: Every time you deal with other people is an opportunity to practice consideration and respectfulness. You can do this in little ways such as a smile, a kind word, a thank you, a nod or a hug.

At first, you may find yourself struggling to master your mind in a more capable way. It may be difficult to think, speak, and act positively - especially when you are handling toxic people. But paying someone back with something bad after being offended would be like splashing each other with dirty waste, and there will never be a true winner.

Actually, a negative attitude can appear to be the logical reaction when you are stuck in a bad situation, but that does not mean you have to adopt one. If you do not give up and make time for input then likely chances your mindset will cultivate more and more positivity. It will be getting easier for you to think about the best possible outcomes in almost everything happening in your life until it finally becomes automatic.

However, despite the fact that random acts of kindness can boost our well-being and happiness, a number of people are still in some doubt about it. They wonder whether the law of cause and effect or karma really works since they see many evil people live so happily and wealthy while good people are less fortune.

It seems to be that way, but if they keep an eye on bad people for long periods of time, they will definitely discover how their evil karma affects their lives. There is a time lag between sowing of seeds and reaping the fruit. Doing a good deed is like growing an apple tree which generally takes three to five years to produce fruits.

What do you have to do while you are waiting for it to reach full maturity? Certainly, you are required to keep watering your tree, fertilizing, and warding off pests.

Such is karma. It needs time to fructify. What you put in this world will be reflected in many aspects of your life's journey without fail. Doing good things is always better than doing bad ones as it not only makes you feel a sense of meaning and reward, but also helps you to improve your spirituality which can move your forward on your path. It will never be a waste of time and effort.

Some people may question your motives and become very reserved about you helping them, but that is totally fine because you cannot please everybody else. Even people who are completely selfless like the Buddha and Jesus Christ had haters.

When you can step into a new way of thinking and a new way of looking at people and things, even what you would call challenges and obstacle, your life will get better in so many ways. So, plant good seeds today and enjoy abundance all around when harvest time comes.

Dear readers,

Thank you for your recent purchase from me. I would be very happy if my readers could learn something new and useful from reading my book.

I would love to hear from you. If you have any comments or concerns with this book I have written, please leave me a review. I would like to offer good product. It is also my goal to continue improving. That is why I value your feedback.

I really do appreciate having you as a reader, and I would like to say thank you for choosing my book.

Best regards,
Talissa Bee

About the Author

Talissa Bee has been involved with books for almost her entire life. She graduated from one of top five universities in Thailand. Her major was Library and Information Science.

In 2010, she started feeling interested in meditation and mindfulness practice after life got her down in many ways – from a broken heart to a financial problem.

In May 2015, she felt aches and pains all over her body and was in intensive care for a week in hospital. She was diagnosed with Guillain Barre syndrome. These experiences made her truly understand how short and uncertain the life was.

She learned how to efficiently overcome obstacle and deal with emotional pain. Now she knows what true happiness is and enjoys letting people know what she has found.

Connect with her at www.twitter.com/beezsan

www.ingramcontent.com/pod-product-compliance
Lightning Source LLC
Chambersburg PA
CBHW021414210526
45463CB00001B/357